PARENTING WITH PURPOSE

Helping Your Teen Embrace and Live Out Their Faith

Dave and Anne Moore

**Parenting with Purpose: Helping Your Teen Embrace
and Live Out Their Faith**

Published by Inscript Books
PO Box 611
Bladensburg, MD 20710-0611

ISBN 978-1-957497-87-7

Published in the United States of America

This book is dedicated to our three
beloved children:
Josh, Neale and Elizabeth

Contents

Prologue

ANNE: Several years ago, Dave and I were out for dinner and ended up discussing how quickly our kids were growing up as they were heading into high school. We saw them becoming more independent, refined in their unique personalities, and trying to figure out how to navigate their faith in a secular environment. We realized that this stage of life required us to shift our parenting from trying to control our kids to coaching and advising them as they navigated their teen years. During this period, we focused on helping them grow as God had designed them, ultimately hoping that they would live out their faith in whatever environment God placed them. This led us to begin teaching a parenting class at our local church, College Park Church in Indianapolis, Indiana. We centered our class discussions on how parents can help guide their Christian children through the pre-teen and teen years to help equip them to engage a secular culture. For many years, we considered writing this book, as the Lord repeatedly placed this topic on our hearts. Yet we hesitated, knowing that it is ultimately God who works in our children's lives. While He calls us to raise them according to Scripture, we do not determine when—or even if—they come to faith. That work belongs to Him alone.

It wasn't until the 2020 pandemic, however, that we were able to put our class material into book form. When the Coronavirus hit the United States, one of our sons was living in New York City, the other was in Chicago, and our daughter was in college. All came home, and for the first time in eight years, we were all together again for an extended period, working and finishing school online.

Several times during quarantine, our kids prodded us to develop a parenting curriculum. It helped to receive their encouragement to do this and to hear from our children how they were now navigating a secular world as adult believers. Living out their faith has not been an easy journey for any of them; however, it has enabled them to be missionally minded as they interact with people from different cultural and religious backgrounds. You will hear from our kids in this book as they share their experiences and give their perspectives.

I am not sure we could have written this book without the unexpected time we were given because of the pandemic, which has impacted our world in deep and difficult ways. Trials are opportunities for refinement, and any hard or helpful experience that conforms us more to Christ and to doing God's will is a blessing. We hope this "fruit" of our time in quarantine will help you prepare your children to be faithful followers of Jesus Christ and to live out their faith in a fallen world.

Introduction

As we raised our children, we benefited greatly from those who had gone before us. It was helpful for us to learn from others' experiences and apply their wisdom to our own parenting. We hope that our experiences helping our children through the teen years will help you formulate what will work best for your family.

As the world is rapidly changing and society's value of biblical principles and its grasp of absolute truth are diminishing, raising Christian kids has become even more challenging and, at times, scary. How do we teach our children to navigate a world that is ambivalent and even hostile to Christianity? How do we prepare our children to engage the culture without succumbing to it?

This book is aimed specifically at parents of children entering the preteen and teenage years. We hope it will equip parents to help their children grow in and refine their faith and to learn how to engage unbelievers in life-changing conversations brought about by the relationships they will have with others. This book will cover strategies for assessing and preparing our children to live out their faith in whatever environment they may find themselves. We will discuss the foundations of parenting, such as:

1. The importance of parents living out their faith
2. The importance of passing on the faith to our kids
3. How to parent and maintain a close relationship with our kids during the teen years
4. Helping our children own their faith and use it to impact the world

5. Help parents develop an action plan for the teen
   years and beyond

Each chapter includes biblical teaching and training, practical examples, and homework for parents to complete and review with your spouse, if you are married. If you are using this book with a group, you are encouraged to share your answers during discussion time. We have designed the application questions for individual parents or couples to consider how they are parenting their children.

It has been said many times that children don't come with an instruction manual. As each of our three children came into our family, we could relate to this statement in so many ways. However, we have found the Bible to be a sufficient and essential guide in raising them.

In light of eternity, our time here on earth is short, so we need to be purposeful in raising our children to know and love the Lord and to live out their faith to a watching and fallen world. There are many things we can provide our children, but, with God's help, the greatest and most enduring thing is a love for Jesus and a desire to advance his kingdom. For many adults, the teen years proved to be the most formative, when they decided what they would build their lives upon. Our prayer is that God will use this workbook to help you encourage your child to build their life upon the sure foundation of Jesus Christ (Matthew 7:24-27).

PARENTING WITH PURPOSE

1

Halftime Adjustment

A Personal Story: Hiking in Rwanda

ANNE: In May of 2019, our family went to Rwanda to visit our cousins who were working in Kigali. While there, we chose to hike Mount Karisimbi, a volcano that is one of the highest peaks in Africa. We were told that this hike was moderately difficult and well-suited for a family of tourists. Our goal was to hike to the base camp, spend the night, and then climb to the volcano's summit the next day.

However, the hike turned out to be different from what we imagined, and the experience became a great parallel for parenting. We entered into the adventure with excitement, but soon realized that it was much harder than expected. About two hours into our hike, as we were trudging uphill through thick trenches of mud, the reality set in that this hike was not moderate but, in fact, strenuous. Even with a lunch break and a few rest stops, it was challenging to keep up with our guides. As we gained altitude and neared the base camp, our need to stop and catch our breath became more frequent. At one point, my husband and I asked our guides if many people our age climbed this volcano. They looked a bit puzzled, so we told them that we were both in our mid-fifties. Their eyes widened in surprise, and one of the guides said that his mom was our age and she would never even consider climbing this volcano! After learning we were old enough to be some of our guides' parents, they began to call me "mama" and my husband, Dave, the "silverback," and sought to take extra care of us.

When we reached the base camp, the view was spectacular. However, nightfall soon approached, and we all began to shiver from being covered in wet mud and exposed to rapidly falling temperatures. Fortunately, a fire and hot beverages awaited us, providing some much-appreciated relief. The base camp was at an elevation of 12,100 feet, which explained why every muscle in my lower body hurt as I sat resting by the fire. Yet, amid the shivers, headaches, and soreness, there was a deeply satisfying feeling that came over me from finishing a very hard journey.

Trudging Through the Mud

As we reflect on our parenting journey now that our kids have reached their twenties, we can look back and acknowledge how difficult it was raising children in the Christian faith that is increasingly counter to the culture in which we live. It required constant instruction, frequent repetition, correction, and consistency. We continually pursued relationships with our children and sought help from the Lord to live out our faith in our family in a way that would, by God's grace, draw our children closer to the Lord. There were many days spent "trudging through the mud" together.

Today, we are grateful to God that all three of our kids have a personal relationship with the Lord and are seeking to follow Jesus. Each of their faith journeys has been rocky and challenging in different ways as they have gone through periods of refinement. It was never a foregone conclusion that they would surrender their lives to Jesus as their Savior and Lord.

The "Garden of Eden" Issue

In the Christian community, we can too easily and incorrectly assume that a child who is raised in a Christian home will automatically choose to follow Jesus. First of all, it is God, not the parents, who determines whether our children will come to faith in Christ. Secondly, Christian parents are far from perfect and do not have the power to ensure that their children will become believers. Parents have sinful natures and will certainly make mistakes; yet, as Christ followers, they will hopefully seek to parent their children in a God-honoring and loving way. Thirdly, even children raised in faithful Christian homes can end up not following Christ. God is perfect, and he gave Adam and Eve everything they needed in the garden, including constant access to Himself. Yet, they still sinned and chose to go their own way. Why then should we be confused or surprised when our children, born of imperfect parents, living in an age of confusion, don't have faith in Jesus, even though they have been taught the scriptures and raised in a Christian home? Our senior pastor, Mark Vroegop, of College Park Church, has often said, "If you think perfect parents naturally leads to perfect children, you have a 'Garden of Eden' issue."

As parents, we must be good stewards of our children and train them up according to the scriptures. We just need to be obedient to do what he calls us to do as parents and trust him with the souls of our children. There will always be areas of growth and challenges ahead for parents and kids alike, because we are works in progress and weighed down by our sinful flesh as long as we are on this earth.

Surrendering Our Parental Struggles Through Prayer

[Anne] As our kids were growing up, there were many times we gave in to worry and even hopelessness. I remember crying myself to sleep one night because I was convinced that one of our sons would grow up to become a convict. He had such a strong will and did not respond well to correction. We butted heads often, and I became exasperated with him. I knew, though, that I could not give up on him and needed to continue to be consistent in how I loved, instructed, and parented him. God continued to work in his life and in mine. Surrendering my struggles and worries to prayer regarding my kids was a huge source of help when days with them were particularly hard. It has always been my prayer that the Lord would just take hold of each one of them and never let them go.

Now that we are recent empty nesters, the daily parts of our parenting journey have faded while the joy of the experience remains. We are now in a consultant role with our grown sons and daughter. This transition is bittersweet. We are excited for them to be living independently, but we miss having them under our roof and the opportunity to interact with them daily. When our children were young, some days seemed to drag on forever, but the years flew by. Looking back, the time we had with them at home seems so fleeting.

Making Changes at Halftime

It is sobering to think that by the time we reach the beginning of the teen years with our kids, over half of the time we have with them under our roof is gone. They will soon be leaving our homes and venturing into the world on their own, and we need to help get them ready to engage the world in a God-honoring way. If you have a hard time imagining your kids ever being ready to leave, or if you notice they are not equipped to engage the world, it's never too late to make changes. In football, teams always have a break at halftime, and it is during those few minutes that they adjust their play and develop a plan for the second half. In the same way, the teen years with your children are a good time to evaluate how things are going and make halftime adjustments. It could be a great opportunity to change your parenting game plan to better help your children prepare to leave home and advance God's kingdom in a secular world.

Being More Purposeful in Our Parenting

Several years ago, we read that an airplane spends over 90% of its time off course when flying towards its destination[1]. The pilot's job is to continually correct the course of the aircraft to ensure it lands where it is supposed to. Our job as parents is similar. We need to have a vision of where we want our children to land as they enter adulthood. This usually means that they will veer left and right as they move towards independence. Many times, we have wanted to either parent on automatic pilot or completely take over the controls, yet this approach with children doesn't help them learn how to fly the plane (or manage their lives). We need to be actively involved in their lives as they enter the teen years, but in a different way than when they were younger. Now we need to be coaches and advisors to them.

This is not a time to have their greatest influences come from broader culture, social media, schoolteachers, or even their youth pastors. Children need their parents. Only parents are called to *"train up their children in the way they should go and when they are old, they will not depart from it"* (Proverbs 22:6). This includes training them up according to scripture, but also recognizing how God has created our kids with unique talents, strengths, struggles, and weaknesses. The teen years are filled with opportunities to lean into our children and be purposeful in how we help guide them.

Below below is a simple framework that has helped us to think about the changing needs as our children mature. The teen years may seem less demanding because the daily physical acts of caring for young children have passed, such as bathing them, feeding them, and changing their diapers. Yet, it is a season in our kids' lives where we need to double down and be more purposeful in our parenting.

---

1   How to Develop Your Personal Mission Statement by Stephen R. Covey, Grand Rapids Press, 2009

It is easy for parents to back off as their kids gain more independence. However, we must realize that during the teen years, our children need us to come alongside them and help them navigate a hard yet very important period of life. Many times, they will not come to us; however, we need to continue lovingly pursuing them as God pursues us.

	Easy to Engage	Harder to Engage
High Need	Toddler	Teen
Lower Need	Grade School	Adult

The ideal time to begin thinking about how to parent our children during this season is before they reach this stage of life. If you are reading this book and your kids are already in the midst of their teen years, it is not too late to be strategic in how you parent them.

Assessing Your Teens' Strengths and Opportunities for Growth

As we saw how quickly our kids were growing up and realized more than ever the challenges they would face in society, we began assessing how we were parenting them to prepare them to engage the world for God's glory. This included observing the strengths and areas for growth of each of our children, then looking for ways to move them outside their comfort zone so that, with God's help, they could persevere and be refined through the challenges they would face.

If we are going to effectively coach our kids through a

difficult second half, we need to have a strong relationship with them. We see throughout the Bible the importance of relationships. Everything begins and ends with our relationship with God and our devotion to Him. Once we have experienced God's overwhelming love and grace, it should naturally pour over into our relationships with others. The most important thing we can do for our kids is to love and pursue them as Christ has loved us.

"The most important thing we can do for our kids is to love and pursue them as Christ has loved us."

As we observe our kids' strengths and weaknesses, we can adjust our parenting to better help them in both categories. If you haven't assessed your kids to parent them with purpose before they are teens, again, it is not too late. If you feel you have blown it or strained your relationships with your kids, God can still work on your relationship with them. Humbly ask God to show you what is necessary to restore your relationship with your children. This should include acknowledging and repenting of past sins towards them, apologizing for the hurts you may have caused them, and asking for their forgiveness. Only when we are restored to our children and have a good relationship with them can we walk alongside them and shepherd them through the teen years into adulthood. We can then help our children grow in their strengths and address their weaknesses, which are profitable for them, for us, and for anyone with whom they interact. We should not be surprised if we need to change how we are parenting them to help them succeed in the "second half" of life.

Halftime Adjustment

Questions for Reflection:

Read Ephesians 5:1-2. Pray through this verse and consider:

1. In what ways am I living this verse out in my parenting?
2. In what ways am I not?
3. Reflect on your parenting approach with your teen and think of examples:
4. Am I patient or easily angered?
5. Am I relational or task-oriented?
6. Am I critical or accepting?
7. Do I have high expectations or low expectations?
8. Do I most often seek to impart truth and justice, or love?
9. Which of the fruit of the Spirit do I need to demonstrate more visibly to my teen?
10. If I am married, how can I help my spouse in our parenting? How can we complement one another?
11. How will I need to change and grow so that God can work through me as I seek to guide my child(ren) during the teen years?
12. How can my spouse or a friend help me with my parenting approach?

Prayer:

Close by praying that God would reveal to you areas of your life and parenting that He wants to change.

2

Loving Relationships are Foundational

Parenting is all about relationships: our walk with the Lord and our relationships with our children. Most of the time, when our relationships or personal lives are off, it can be traced back to our walk with the Lord. It is so easy for us to navigate life relying on our own wisdom and strength and to approach parenting in the same manner. When challenges arise and our self-reliance fails, we can spiral into an overwhelming feeling of inadequacy because parenting is such an important yet difficult task. However, God wants to use the challenges of parenting to work in us and make us more dependent upon Him. One of the great revelations we had while raising teens was that, while our focus was on how God was changing and shaping our children, we realized He was doing the same to us. Many times, we had to repent of sinful patterns and examine the idols of our own hearts revealed through the challenges of parenting our children.

In parenting, it is important to remember that discipleship occurs best within the context of a relationship. Think of a time when you grew the most spiritually. There was likely a Godly person in your life who pointed you to the truth of God's Word and helped you grow. That is the pattern we see throughout scriptures – our spiritual growth occurs when we are in the Word, in community, and in Christ-centered relationships. As our children mature into young adults, we need to continue our relationship with them but transition from "control and protection" to "guidance and mentoring."

The Main Focus of Parenting Teens

As parents, we have found that there are three main things we need to focus on during our kids' teen years.

Model Jesus's Love to Your Teen

The first area that we need to focus on is modeling Jesus' love in our relationship with our kids. 1 Thessalonians 2:8 (ESV) says, "*So, being affectionately desirous of you, we were ready to share with you not only the gospel of God but also our own selves, because you had become very dear to us*". When our children face the challenges and loneliness that can arise in the teen years, they must experience our unconditional love and feel like home can be a safe place. It needs to be a "locker room," where they can get bandaged up and coached before they go back into the world. It is important that we continually pursue a relationship with our kids. Every evening before bed, we told our kids that we loved them, then we prayed with them and hugged and kissed them goodnight. They need that affirmation and love as much now as they did when they were little.

Help Your Teen Build the Foundation of THEIR life upon Jesus Christ.

The second area of focus is to help our children build the foundation of THEIR lives upon Jesus Christ (Luke 6:47-49). For some of us, this may be evangelistic; for others, it is focused on discipleship. We should take opportunities to study our child for the good of his or her soul. We need to remember that, in the Bible, the model for spiritual leadership is shepherding sheep, not driving cattle. We need to model and lead, but only God can do the work. The journey needs to be our child's. As parents, our primary goal is to point our children to Christ in the hope that they will become His disciples.

3. Help Your Teen Gain Christian Maturity

The third area is to help our children mature when they encounter hardships. In the book, *How Children Succeed: Grit, Curiosity and the Hidden Power of Character* [2], Paul Tough discusses two stages of development in which parents have the greatest impact. The first is birth through infancy, and the second is adolescence. The first stage requires protection, whereas the second requires learning how to grow through adversity. Our children need to learn how to solve problems and deal with the difficulties they encounter, rather than being shielded. We need to be there as parents to guide and support them through that process. We believe the scripture writer James, in Chapter 1:2-4, when he says that trials perfect our faith. It is hard to witness our children enduring challenges, yet it is the necessary path to Christian maturity.

One of the most important things we can do as parents during the teen years is to lean *in to* our kids rather than step *away* from them. Teenagers want their independence and should be given opportunities to increasingly exercise it responsibly; therefore, leaning in to our kids does not mean we hover over them or micromanage their lives. It means that we make ourselves available for the unexpected times they want to talk, which for us was usually late at night. We also need to observe their body language and behavior in order to draw them out or to just give them a reassuring hug without saying a word. Leaning in means being attuned to our teens' signals that they may need us, even when they don't explicitly express it.

For example, one of our children went through a period when they lacked joy because they had been pursuing

---

2   Tough, P. (2012). How children succeed: Grit, curiosity, and the hidden power of character. Houghton Mifflin Harcourt.

worldly things. They were living in ways that were incongruent with how God made them, and, in addition to lacking joy, they became withdrawn. This was such a change in their demeanor that we made sure we were around them often, loving them unconditionally and doing things with them, which opened the door to asking them specific questions about our observations. Eventually, they confessed that they were miserable because they were not pursuing the Lord and had neglected their relationship with Him in favor of earthly things that proved completely unsatisfying. They repented of this and sought to make the Lord their main priority once again. Soon, we began to see peace and joy re-emerge in our teenager. After that, our teen still struggled with living for the Lord, but that moment was a turning point in their sanctification and an opening for us to encourage them in their pursuit of the Lord.

Building a Relationship with Your Teen

Several things have helped us build relationships with our children throughout the years:

<u>Spend Quality Time with Your Teen - and Listen</u>

Quality time starts by spending time with them, listening to them, and getting to know their unique characteristics. We should learn about their interests and actively engage them in these activities. We need to be available for the unexpected moments when they want to share what is on their hearts. Relationships and discipleship with our kids occur through the many exchanges we have with them every day. Several years ago, Frank Bruni wrote this in the New York Times:

> "I know how my 80-year-old father feels
> about dying, religion and God not because I
> scheduled a discreet encounter to discuss all
> of that with him. I know because I happened
> to be in the passenger seat of his car when

such thoughts were on his mind, and when, for whatever unforeseeable reason, he felt comfortable articulating them."

. . .

"It was on a run one morning that my oldest niece described, as she'd never done for me before, the joys, frustrations and contours of her relationships with her parents, her two sisters and her brother. Why this information tumbled out of her then, with pelicans overheard and sweat slicking our foreheads, I can't tell you. But I can tell you that I'm even more tightly bonded with her now, and that's not because of some orchestrated, contrived effort to plumb her emotions. It's because I was present. It's because I was there"[3].

We need to be there for our teens. We should empathize with them and really take the time to understand what they are going through.

Show Respect to Your Teen

Make sure that you show your teen respect even when they are being childish. Our kids tend to rise or fall to our expectations, so if we talk down to them, they will likely respond to us in a manner commensurate with how we are treating them.

Invest Time in Your Teens' Interests

Help them find something they are good at and encourage them in it. Even if it is an activity in which you have no knowledge, interest, or aptitude, it should be important to you if it is important to your child.

When one of our sons was in middle school, he began playing lacrosse. [DAVE]: I knew nothing about lacrosse but took an extra lacrosse head that my son had, attached it to a

---

3   Frank Bruni, The Myth of Quality Time, New York Times, 2015

broom handle, and began throwing with him. We had some great times together, learning how to throw lacrosse balls and debriefing. A year later, my son bought me a lacrosse stick, which I still have and use when the boys are home.

Give Your Teen Unconditional Love, Which Fosters Honesty and Trust

One of the most important things that kids need to feel is that you are in their corner, loving them unconditionally. If they feel this love, you have earned the right to speak into their lives, saying almost anything, but you really do need to seek their best interest when counseling them. Never use their trust to manipulate them into doing what you want. Always keep their secrets and never betray that trust. Never forget that it is a precious thing to be the confidant of your child.

Have FUN!

Be sure to have times of fun with your kids, make memories, and create traditions.

A Personal Story: "Happy Dog"

DAVE: We have heard from two of our three kids about their disappointment about not having a dog in our home. Due to allergies, a decent amount of travel, and a disastrous experience with a dog when we were first married, we decided not to add one to our family. Anne saw that our kids were disappointed that they didn't have a dog, so she pretended to be one when they were little. At night, as we tucked them into bed, "Happy Dog" would appear. She would come into their rooms crawling on all fours, wagging her pretend tail, and panting like a dog. Then she would pounce on them and snuggle up close to them. They loved it and would often ask for visits from "Happy Dog."

The kids also knew Anne was making dinner when they heard Motown playing in the kitchen. It was common for them to wander in and see their mom dancing while she cooked. Often, the kids would join in, and dancing became a spontaneous family activity in the kitchen. And it still is to this day, when they come home.

When our kids have shared what they appreciate about their childhood, they have said it is memories and traditions like these, as well as other relationship-building activities we did with them, such as throwing the football, building forts, having indoor and outdoor picnics, or putting on plays together. All of these little acts communicated, "You are important to me, and I like spending time with you."

Cover Your Teen with Grace

We need to remember how difficult the adolescent years can be and give our kids a measure of grace. This does not mean allowing them to get away with selfish behavior or violations against God's law. At times, it means bringing grace and calm to an emotion-filled young person. Do a self-check and gauge where you are in balancing grace and discipline. Each of us tends to be either a "grace person" or a "truth person," but Jesus Christ is both truth and grace. He is to be our example.

Loving Relationships are Foundational

Questions for Reflection:

1. Where am I relationally with my teen right now? How am I taking the time to invest in their life and the things they care about?
2. What can I do to pursue a relationship with my teen? (list actions for each child based upon their interests)
3. If I am married, discuss how I can work together with my spouse as a unified team in raising our teen.

Prayer:

Pray for your relationship with your teen(s). Pray that God would strengthen your relationship with them and reveal ways in which you can connect with them.

3

Having Godly Objectives for Your Teen

Throughout the many years of parenting our children, one of the Bible passages that we kept re-visiting was Deuteronomy 6:1-9:

"Now this is the commandment—the statutes and the rules —that the Lord your God commanded me to teach you, that you may do them in the land to which you are going over, to possess it, 2 that you may fear the Lord your God, you and your son and your son's son, by keeping all his statutes and his commandments, which I command you, all the days of your life, and that your days may be long. 3 Hear therefore, O Israel, and be careful to do them, that it may go well with you, and that you may multiply greatly, as the Lord, the God of your fathers, has promised you, in a land flowing with milk and honey. 4 "Hear, O Israel: The Lord our God, the Lord is one. 5 You shall love the Lord your God with all your heart and with all your soul and with all your might. 6 And these words that I command you today shall be on your heart. 7 You shall teach them diligently to your children, and shall talk of them when you sit in your house, and when you walk by the way, and when you lie down, and when you rise. 8 You shall bind them as a sign on your hand, and they shall be as

frontlets between your eyes. 9 You shall write them on the doorposts of your house and on your gates."

These verses served as a good reminder of the command we have been given as parents to instruct the next generation in the ways of the Lord. In this passage, Moses reminds the children of Israel of the need to teach future generations about Yahweh and all that God had done in delivering his people.

The first point that we observe in this passage is that discipleship must begin with us as parents. We cannot delegate this task to the youth group leaders or to a Christian school. While these can be real blessings, it is uniquely the privilege and responsibility that God has given to parents. In verses 5 and 6, the word "you(r)" appears seven times:

"And <u>you</u> shall love the Lord <u>your</u> God with all <u>your</u> heart and with all <u>your</u> soul and with all <u>your</u> strength. These commandments that I give <u>you</u> today are to be on <u>your</u> hearts."

From this passage, we see that God's first desire is that parents are, first and foremost, lovers and followers of Christ. One of the most important things we can do for our children is authentically model the Christian life. If you have ever led others, you know that it is very hard to take someone to a level you have never been yourself. This does not mean we need to be perfect, but it does mean we need to love the Lord with all our hearts and follow his statutes. One thing you have likely observed in other families is that the kids often love what their parents love and are passionate about what they are passionate about. If I am passionate about camping, my children will likely love it, too.

Modeling the Christian life is not presenting to our kids a perfect Christian life, but showing that we are serious about obeying the call of Christ and repenting when we fail. Having a heart of humility and acknowledging that we are flawed sinners can have the greatest impact on our children. Many times, we have apologized to our kids when we have sinned against them or others. We do so by confessing what we did to sin against them and then ask them to forgive us. If we do not model humility and repentance to our children, we risk modeling hypocrisy.

We have known families where the one parent, who professes to be a Christian, is also the most difficult person to interact with in the family. This person has lived a life where the faith professed has been a poor witness to the family. A parent who lives a deceitful life can negatively impact the children to the point where they want nothing to do with Christianity. In this situation, could God still call them to Himself? Absolutely. But the way that a person lives out their faith has a profound, even eternal, influence on those closest to them, especially their family. When done well, the impact can be life-changing. When done poorly, the results can be devastating.

Parents need to continually seek God, learn His Word, and humbly live out their faith in the Lord in order to bring honor to God as they parent their children. They are to reflect His character, resulting in an environment that is loving, safe, and winsome for God's kingdom.

The second point that the Deuteronomy passage makes is that we are to "teach them (God's commands) diligently to our children." In addition to modeling, we are to instruct our children. We see this in the ministry of Christ as He both modeled God the Father and taught His disciples. This verse says that we are to instruct "diligently." Passing on the faith to the next generation requires intentionality. Any successful endeavor, whether business, civic, or athletic, requires a plan. What plans and efforts have you laid out to instruct your children about the Lord? Life during the teen years is full of activities, and it goes by very fast. Without a spiritual plan and sacrifices to see it through, it will not happen.

The third parenting principle is found in verse seven. In this verse, we see that instruction is to be part of the natural flow of life. We are to talk about God and his law throughout our day. Moses lists every posture that we should assume throughout our daily routine. The idea is that biblical instruction is to be continual. We will never accomplish this by running from one activity to the next, being distracted by our phones, or being absent from our children too often. We need to be fully present and living life with them.

Keeping our Eyes on the Target

Let's examine Psalm 127 (NIV):

> [1] *"Unless the Lord builds the house, the builders labor in vain. Unless the Lord watches over the city, the guards stand watch in vain.*
> [2] *In vain you rise early and stay up late, toiling for food to eat— for he grants sleep to[a] those he loves.*
> [3] *Children are a heritage from the Lord, offspring a reward from him.*
> [4] *Like arrows in the hands of a warrior are children born in one's youth.*
> [5] *Blessed is the man whose quiver is full of them. They will not be put to shame when they contend with their opponents in court."*

In this psalm, we read that children are to be like arrows, ready to penetrate their target. Arrows must first be aimed at a target and then released. Setting goals helps us refine the actions needed to reach the target. What goals do you have for your kids? What is the battle you are launching them into? We have found that this release is not a one-time event but an ongoing process throughout your children's lives. It is most often the small steps taken that accumulate and launch them into adulthood rather than one big leap.

The direction in which an arrow flies is based on the guidance of the archer. In the same way, the path on which a child is launched should be shaped by the parents and ultimately determined by the Lord. Our children will face cultural influence, peer pressure, and temptations that can impede their trajectory. Yet, with God's help, we can influence the path they take.

As we aim them toward a life of following Jesus, we should seek additional people who will support their spiritual journey. We also need to help our kids tackle the daily challenges they face by talking openly with them about their struggles and temptations and by helping them navigate those challenges.

Sometimes it is helpful to begin the journey with the end in mind. Imagine for a minute the day your child graduates from high school and then leaves home to begin a new chapter in their life. How do you want to equip them before they leave home? What faith do you want to impart to help shape the trajectory of their lives? For our children, we developed several "targets" for them to pursue, and encouraged them, by God's help and grace, to reach them.

Helping Your Teen Develop a Relationship with Jesus

The first target was to help them as much as possible develop a personal, vibrant relationship with Jesus Christ. This begins by observing whether our kids really have an authentic relationship with Jesus Christ as their Lord and Savior. While only God knows definitively one's standing before Him, we can look for evidence of faith in our children. The things we looked for in our children's lives were the fruit of the Spirit (*But the fruit of the Spirit is love, joy, peace, patience, kindness, goodness, faithfulness, gentleness, self-control; against such things there is no law.* Galatians 5:22-23), an internally generated desire for Him, and humility.

Helping Your Teen Develop an Understanding of Theology

The second target was to help our teens develop a

theologically informed view of the world. We tried to impart theological truths to our children at an early age that would inform their views of the world and their decision-making. A mistake many parents make is underestimating the depth of theological truths that young children can understand. This causes some children to be exposed to a very shallow, incomplete model of Christianity rather than the glorious truths of God. We sought to impart these truths through regular times of family devotions, scripture memory, and hymns. However, we imparted much of our teaching about God's truth by sharing our struggles and by having our kids see us process life's joys and trials in light of the promises of God. Our kids saw our faith and theology lived out as we went through trials and difficulties. We also found it very helpful to talk with our teens about the views of the world they were encountering in school or popular culture and how those attitudes compare to the truth of scripture.

<u>Helping Your Teens Develop a Missional Mindset</u>

The third target was to encourage our kids to formulate a missional mindset. We have listed it third because it should be an outcome of the first two targets. If your child is already following Jesus and has a strong theological grounding, they should begin to serve others where God has placed them. Encourage them to seek out opportunities to serve others. It could be helping to teach a Sunday school class, witnessing to their classmates, or serving the homeless, for example.

It is important to have these three targets in mind as you parent through the teen years. You will quickly experience the pull of the world and the many demands on your children, such as academics, athletics, clubs, jobs, applying for scholarships, college entrance requirements, etc. While these can be good things, they are not of primary importance.

Barriers to These Targets

Some barriers or challenges can hinder our ability to focus on these three important aims for our kids.

Focusing on Behavior and Not the Heart

First, we need to focus on the root issues in our children's lives rather than the fruit. It is easy for parents to focus on their children's outward behavior rather than their hearts. As long as they are doing what is right and socially acceptable, we can wrongly assume that their souls are thriving.

Leaning In to the Hard Things

Second, by the time our children are teenagers, we are tired and tempted to back off and not be as involved. It is tough going back into the "high school world" and coming alongside our kids to help them navigate a toxic friend group or continual peer pressure. As hard as it was, we were thankful when our kids discussed with us the challenges they were having with peers at school. At the same time, there were moments when we grew very weary of how our children were hurting and found ourselves reliving memories of these difficult seasons in our own lives. We often wondered what was more difficult—going through the teen years as a young person or as a parent. It is hard when you see your child suffering, and you feel limited in your ability to fix the situation. This causes many parents to want to "outsource" parenting and avoid leading and guiding their children during the teen years. Conversely, it can also tempt a parent to step into the middle of the situation and take over, removing whatever is hard for the child. This may ease the child's immediate struggle, but it ultimately hinders their growth and their ability to navigate and resolve challenging people and situations on their own. We need to be approachable and authentic with our kids to help them navigate challenging situations while under our roof. In our home, we wanted our kids to learn how to work through difficult issues they faced in their daily lives and understand that struggles are a normal part of life. They learned to work through tough challenges with our help, so that when they left home, they would not be shocked or ill-equipped to respond to a postmodern Christian world.

Guarding Against Prideful Motives

Third, parenting can become all about us when we let our own pride get in the way. Many parents want their kids to be successful in order to fulfill their own selfish desires. They push their kids and will boast about their achievements to others, whether their child is the starting football player, an honor student, or just got into a prestigious college. Some cases involve parents trying to relive their high school dreams through their teens. We have seen too many overly pushy parents in the athletic stands or behind the stage, yelling at their kids. As parents, we do not want to place the burden on our children to perform and achieve for our sake. Too much parental pressure can turn kids into "performance machines," earning their parents' approval through their accomplishments. The love and acceptance they experience from their parents are conditional and based on achievement, so children will quickly learn to produce what their parents expect in order to feel loved and accepted. They will hear their Christian parents profess that faith in Christ is the most important part of their lives, but they will actively experience that what really matters most to Mom and Dad are worldly achievements. Children will see the hypocrisy of this narrative in their parents and rebel against this pressure by withdrawing or acting out.

High school should be a time for our kids to explore their God-given gifts and passions. As parents, we should be coming alongside our kids to help them accomplish the plan God has for them, not making our kids "trophy kids" to impress our friends. Instead, we need to show unconditional love for our children and encourage them to pursue God's vision for their lives, not our own idols.

<u>A Personal Story: When There Are No Lanes</u>

[Dave:] When each of our boys turned twelve years old, I would do a short triathlon with them, followed by an Entrance into Manhood party. As they prepared for the race, I talked with them about how much harder an open-water swim is than swimming laps in a lane pool, where lane lines help swimmers swim in a straight line. It also has lane dividers to help prevent the swimmer from drifting too far off course. An open body of water does not have the same built-in guidance and controls. This is a helpful analogy for parents to consider when thinking about raising children. Our children's early years are a lot like lane swimming. As parents, we should create clear rules and an environment that keeps our children focused on the Lord. The teen years tend to be more like open-water swimming. Open-water swimming has no set markers or lane lines. The key to success in open-water swimming is to learn "sighting," in which the swimmer finds a fixed point on the opposite shore and swims toward it. This fixed point on the shore helps orient the swimmer, despite water splashing around them and being kicked by other swimmers. The whole experience of an open-water swim can be quite disorienting the first several times.

We need to understand the challenges of being "in the water" and be there to talk when our kids need to, such as when they've been "kicked in the face" or have "swallowed a mouthful of water." We also still need some boundaries and clear guidelines, but the goal is for them to grow in maturity and in their pursuit of Christ. At times, discipline and consequences are necessary, but the goal should be to learn from the failures as part of the refinement process in growing toward maturity in Christ.

Faith During Trials

One of our sons tends to overcommit and say "yes" to too many people and opportunities. During his senior year in high school, he was concurrently captain of his lacrosse team, participated in the school play, and had a senior capstone project, in addition to a challenging academic load. These activities had our son running from one thing to the next, unable to fully commit to any of them. He quickly realized that he had overcommitted and came to us. We stressed to him his need to keep his commitments and to persevere despite the overwhelming pressure he was under as a consequence of saying "yes" to too many opportunities. It also gave us a chance to help our son recognize his desire to please others and seek their approval, which, in turn, led to a crazy spring semester that was exhausting and not enjoyable for him.

This example is familiar to many teens, but God may bring trials into your children's lives that are truly devastating....

As parents, we need to remind ourselves that the normative Christian life is not easy or pain-free. Rather, the scriptures say that our lives will have pain and suffering. We need to trust God when he brings hard trials into our children's lives. Many times, we buy into a gospel of self-fulfillment and comfort versus a ministry of self-denial and suffering. We must remind ourselves that Christ calls us to die to our own desires. As 20th-century German theologian Dietrich Bonhoeffer said, "When God bids a man to come follow Him, he bids him to die (paraphrased)." [4]

We found it helpful to regularly ask ourselves if we were seeking *God's* will or *our* will for our kids. During particularly hard times, it was helpful to remember God's will for believers undergoing challenges in the Bible. Namely, it was to bring them into maturity in Christ rather than

---

4   Dietrich Bonhoeffer, The Cost of Discipleship, trans. R. H. Fuller, rev. ed. (New York: Touchstone, 1995), 44.

make them happy in the moment. God uses trials in our lives to produce maturity. As James 1:2-4 (ESV) says: *"Count it all joy, my brothers, when you meet trials of various kinds, for you know that the testing of your faith produces steadfastness. And let steadfastness have its full effect, that you may be perfect and complete, lacking in nothing."*

Social Isolation

Our kids will have times when they are standing alone as they follow Christ. As parents, we don't want this for our kids; we want them to be liked by others and not have to suffer. In our experience, every one of our kids has been excluded from a peer group at some point because they didn't conform to the group's ideals. They have been "labeled" because of their faith, and it was hard for them. As parents, we need to realize that if our kids walk with Christ in their teen years, they will be alone many times. Parents, this becomes a faith issue. Is God big enough to hold our kids in His hand amid a sinful world? Does hardship really produce godliness?

We need to seek a bigger vision for our kids. It is easy to focus on daily challenges or think about minimizing bad behavior. We believe that success in the teen years is *not* just about good grades and avoiding bad behavior. It is about being sold out for Christ and living in such a way that it is clear that He is our treasure, not the world or the acceptance of others.

Having Godly Objectives for Your Teen

Questions for Reflection:

1. What is my natural parenting tendency towards my children in the teen years (over-control or hands-off)? Which extreme can I most relate to? Do I want to run and hide until the teen years are over, or try to control my children's every behavior?
2. What are ways I can grow in my trust in God and reliance on Him during this season of life?
3. What are some ways my spouse or a friend could help balance my parenting approach?
4. What goals do I have for my children as they transition to adulthood in the area of:

   - Spiritual growth
   - Academic/Wisdom
   - Character qualities

Prayer:

Close in prayer by asking God to reveal any wrong motives you have in parenting your children. Spend some time praying that God would work in your child's heart and grow them into the men/women God desires them to be.

4

Creating a Supportive Home Environment During Turbulent Teen Years

Let's face it, the teen years are difficult. As parents, we need to make our home a place where our children can escape the pressures of this world, be themselves, and experience that Christ is real. This creates an important environment for authentic discipleship. So much of discipleship is modeled in day-to-day home life. God does not call us to be perfect parents but rather to seek and follow a perfect Savior.

Prioritizing Jesus Among the Distractions

Yet, like many other challenging seasons in our lives, the teen years can be a time of great growth. Our teens are hit from all sides by the things of this world. They must deal with social pressures from peers, the obsession with social media, and the pursuit of worldly pleasures and entertainment. When managed well, these activities can bring enjoyment to daily life. But when they are valued and pursued above all else, they can lure our kids into a world that seeks to claim and control them. We must counteract the self-promotion, absorption, and fleeting fulfillment that worldly diversions can bring by pointing our children to Christ. He is the source who is life-giving, lasting, and ultimately fulfilling.

As David Michael, our friend and president of Truth 78, says: "We must surrender all worldly claims upon our children's lives in the hope that they will belong wholly to the Lord forever." Godly parenting must begin by recognizing that our children are ultimately the Lord's, not ours. We must continually and fully surrender control of our parenting to the Lord and trust His sovereign plan for our children as we parent them in accordance with Scripture. Having this foundation is vital for children who are becoming adults themselves and who, many times, make very different choices than we would.

We first tried to model this for our children by prioritizing serving God rather than seeking our own pleasure. We have found that parenting begins with self-examination. Parents should ask themselves hard questions, such as:

- How can I encourage my teen to prioritize Christ when I am filling my own life with many other distractions?
- How can I expect my teen to make good media decisions when I am watching movies with questionable content?

The second thing we tried to do was help them begin making their own decisions about what they will do and what they will be involved in. We felt like high school was a great chance to do that before they moved out of the house. Without being overbearing, we tried to engage with our children in making choices informed by their faith. Like so many things during the teen years, it is about helping them form their own convictions informed by the scriptures rather than trying to control them.

The Role of Fathers and Father Figures

[Dave]: Fathers play a vital role in setting the tone in the home. Scripture is very clear that fathers are to lead the spiritual training in their homes. The scriptures caution fathers against provoking their children to anger (Ephesians 6:4). We need to realize that how we lead (positively or negatively) greatly affects our family. As fathers, we do not want to create an oppressive home environment where our kids feel like they will never measure up to our demanding expectations. Fathers and mothers also should not be controlling and overprotective, as it hinders our children from ever taking risks and learning from their mistakes. Children will never become independent thinkers and leaders if they are always told what to think, say, and do. If a child's father is not present or involved in building your child's faith, pray about finding a Godly male role model to help guide your child and help fulfill God's plan for how a family shapes a child.

Be Aware of the Influence of Your Upbringing

In Romans 12:1-2, Paul exhorts us not to conform to the pattern of this world but to be transformed by renewing our minds through the scriptures. As we begin to approach the teen years with our children, we need to recognize the many influences that could shape how we parent. We will be shaped both positively and negatively by our family of origin and by the way we were parented growing up. We found it helpful to reflect as a couple on the positive things from our childhoods that we wanted to bring into our parenting, and on what, by God's grace, we did not want to repeat with our children due to generational sin. Whether you feel you had a wonderful or terrible example growing up, we all have the perfect example of our Heavenly Father and the power of the Holy Spirit to enable us to raise godly teens.

God's Instruction to Parents

One of God's unforeseen purposes for us as parents during our children's teen years is our own sanctification. Our job as parents during this time is not to "fix our kids," but to help with their continued growth and sanctification.

We were surprised to learn that God had planned as much sanctifying work in our own lives as He did for our kids. We went into the teen years thinking about all the areas in which our kids needed to grow, only to realize that God had the same thoughts and desires for us. We found that many times the things that frustrated us about our children were the same things we struggled with. We would often get on our kids about prideful tendencies and self-centered behaviors, only to have God immediately convict us of that same pattern in our own lives. We see why the scriptures encourage us to reflect on ourselves before we confront someone in sin. The habit of examining our own hearts helped us approach our children with better discernment when we had to address the sin in their lives.

The Foundational Role of Parents

Because of the difficulty of the teen years, it is easy to fall into one of two ditches: backing off or controlling. Backing off means failing to be involved in our kids' lives, letting them "figure it out." Given the busyness of life, it is easy to feel like we don't have the time or energy to devote to parenting our teen. It can be easier to hand off the teaching and discipleship of our children to a church youth group or Christian school. Many justify this approach by saying, "I'm not a pastor" or "I can't answer the questions my child has." Whenever you are unable to answer a question from your teen, you and your teen can search for the answer together. Please remember that a youth group leader or teacher can never replace the invaluable role you have as a parent. If you ask anyone who ministers to youth, they will tell you how vital parenting and a healthy home life are for teens. The time you spend during their teen years as a parent is an indispensable role that only you can fill. While it requires sacrifice, remember that you are building a relationship for life.

Another tendency we must fight is to parent out of fear, trying to control our kids' every move. We certainly understand parents' concern about the many evils in this world and the desire to wisely protect our children. This can be a very natural tendency when the depravity of the world fosters a desire to protect our children from its many evils. While this may work in grade school, controlling your junior high and high school kids does not work. In fact, it often backfires, and children can become secretive and try to evade Mom and Dad's control. God wants our kids to learn from the mistakes they make as they grow up. If kids live in an environment where mistakes and failures are not tolerated, they will not learn. God wants us to help our children in their walk and sanctification. As believing parents, we need to remember that God is sovereign. He will be with us even when we walk through the valley of the shadow of death.

Avoiding Over-Scheduling Your Teen

It is also very easy to succumb to the societal expectations of those around us. It is easy to feel like your kids are falling behind if they are not in a crazy number of activities or building their college resumes. While we wanted our kids to try a lot of things, we tried to resist the trend of having them booked every minute. It can often be seen as a badge of honor ("Look at how busy my kids are!"), but we found it really difficult to build relationships and mentor our kids while frequently running around to club sports, music, or dance lessons. Overly busy kids can descend into production mode, in which they begin to believe that "My worth is in what I produce."

Our True Identity is as a Child of God

Our kids need to see God's unconditional love in us. Our pastor, Mark Vroegop, shared a story one Sunday:

"A few years back, I was driving one of my sons home from his basketball game, and he was crying.

He's a great basketball player, but on this day, his performance was less than stellar. As a result, he was crushed. After doing my best to comfort him by listening to him and reminding him that his game was not nearly as bad as he thought, he told me plainly, 'Dad, I played terrible.' I said, 'I know you don't think you played well, but why does not playing well make you so sad?' He said with tremendously keen self-awareness, 'Because I'm a basketball player. That's who I am.' Somewhere along the way, he had concluded, due to his success on the basketball court over the years, that his self-worth and value as a person were inextricably tied to his achievements as a basketball player. If he were a good basketball player, he would matter. If he wasn't, then he didn't matter. To him, a bad game was more than a bad game. It was a direct assault on his identity."

He needed to be reminded that his true identity is as a child of God. Like all of us, our children need to be reminded that their identity is in Christ, not in what they accomplish or who they know.

Navigating through the teen years is difficult and a time of insecurity for our kids. They need parents to support them and to help guide them through these difficult years. They do not need parents to layer on a bunch of unnecessary parental expectations.

Thoughts on Social Media

One area that has changed significantly since we were growing up is the role of technology and social media. While technology can have positive impacts, there have now been many studies on the negative effects of social media, especially upon youth. As parents, we need to carefully think about the impact it will have on the home. The following are a few approaches to managing technology with our children in the home:

Technology Should Not Isolate Individual Family Members

Technology should help to bring the family together, not separate us. One year, one of our sons really wanted an iPod and headphones to listen to music. We were worried that his walking around the house with music blaring in his headphones could negatively impact family dynamics. We talked to him and shared our concerns (with which he did not completely agree) and our desire that technology bring us together as a family. We told him we would not get those for his birthday. Instead, we asked if he would like a video projector that we could put in the basement to watch movies as a family. We then worked on this project and spent many evenings enjoying family movies together. Years later, he said he was glad we had not agreed to buy him an iPod and that it was helpful to him not to be overly dependent on technology.

Parents Must Model Respectful Technology Etiquette

As parents, we need to model good behavior regarding technology. Many times, parents model addictive behaviors with their phones, looking at and scrolling through social media, while ignoring people and letting calls and texts interrupt their conversations with the people right in front of them. While there are certainly times when work emails or important texts need to be addressed promptly, many parents are guilty of getting lost in technology and modeling this dissociative behavior to their kids. We need to use technology so our kids see it as a useful tool, not as a way to control our lives. When the family is together, work really hard to be truly present for one another. This action on your part will communicate to your family, "I value you more than what is on my phone."

Reserve the Right to Restrict the Utilization of Technology

There have been times when we had to have our kids put their phones in a large bowl as they came into the house and leave them there while they did homework, or when we all took a break from technology as a family. Technology has been designed to be entertaining and addictive. It is hard for any of us not to get distracted by it. If needed, parental controls limiting usage hours can also be implemented through most mobile phone carriers. We must help our children learn how to set boundaries between the time they devote to technology and the time they spend with people and other God-given activities in their lives.

Meal Time is Sacred – NO Technology Allowed!

Technology is not allowed to detract from family time or meals. It is truly sad to see a family out to eat at a restaurant, each person engrossed in their phone and ignoring the others. We believe that life is far too busy not to have some time during the day to put down our screens and have meaningful conversations together as a family. This may require us to "up our game" on dinner time conversation as a family. Asking family members to bring fun topics to the dinner table for family discussion is also helpful.

It's been disturbing to see a decline in social skills among today's children due to the widespread adoption of technology. The lack of face-to-face interactions has left many young people inept at conversing intelligently and meaningfully with others, even at maintaining good eye contact. One of the greatest gifts we can give our children is the ability to connect with others. These are vital social and career skills that we can teach our children.

Technology is a Privilege, Not a Right

Our children need to learn to use technology responsibly. In agreeing to allow our kids to use phones and computers for personal use, we had an understanding with them that we would monitor both the time spent and the sites they visited on these devices. We had the codes to our kids' phones and would set parental controls. We also had the right to request to see what they were doing on their phones. This was not to exert control over our kids, but to help keep them accountable.

Note: Over the past few years, several informative studies and books have been published on this topic. One book that we found particularly helpful was *12 Ways Your Phone is Changing You,* by Tony Reinke. [5]

Reflection on the importance of a supportive home environment by our youngest child, Elizabeth

I am very blessed to have grown up in a loving, Christ-centered home where the Gospel was regularly demonstrated to me through my relationship with my parents. As a little girl, I was known as the "velcro" child, sticking to my mom like glue. I was timid and quiet, and often relied on my older brothers to speak on my behalf. From an early age, I learned that my parents were always a unit. When I asked my mom if I could sleepover at a friend's house, she would have me talk to my dad first before giving me an answer. Even though I did not understand this at the time, I quickly grew to appreciate this unity between my parents. As a child, I tried to perfectly obey rules and desired to honor my parents. I was fearful of getting in trouble and would avoid most actions that led to consequences. I had a sensitive conscience and confessed everything to my parents, even when I had not done anything wrong.

However, as I got into middle school, I found it more difficult to open up to my parents and began seeking advice from others. Around this time, my parents realized I needed to grow in my level of perseverance. A common theme in my life as a child and teenager was my resistance to getting outside of my comfort zone. I was comfortable with what was familiar in my life and wanted my circum-

---

5   Reinke, Tony. Twelve Ways Your Phone is Changing You, Crossway, 2017

stances to remain unchanged. At the age of thirteen, my parents transferred me to a new middle school. When I entered this more academically rigorous school, my dad challenged me to join the cross-country team, knowing that it would require me to grow in perseverance. I did not have a Christ-honoring attitude during that season and was very frustrated by having to run many miles each day with a team. Despite my negative attitude, my dad remained steadfast in his demeanor and love towards me. He did special things to encourage me after practices, such as getting me apple cider slushies, taking me to get bagels, or even sharing tips for getting better at running. He never responded to my attitude in kind but instead rose above it and displayed, through his calm demeanor, the love that our heavenly Father has for us.

As I entered high school, my parents would pursue me by taking me out for coffee or lunch dates about once a month. I thoroughly enjoyed this time with each of my parents, and this simple gesture made me feel extremely special amid my teenage insecurities. My dad read books with me and did a great job of pursuing me. My mom and I have always been super close, and I was thankful to have her as a mentor, mom, and best friend all wrapped into one. Like many teens, I desired to feel seen and understood. This investment helped foster a deep and close relationship with both of my parents. They took the time to understand my hobbies, my relationship with the Lord, and my relationship with others.

While I was at college, I went through a period when I was not living for the Lord. My faith was put to the test like never before. While I knew what was right, I wanted the approval of others and desired to fit in with my peers. I am thankful to the Lord that he protected me even when I was being foolish. My parents remained steadfast in their love for me. I tried to hide my actions from them at times, but they knew me well enough to see my lack of peace and know that I was not right with the Lord. I grew weary of the empty pursuit of man's approval and of living for myself. I desired to turn away from my sinful lifestyle. Rather than trying to hide my sin, I brought my parents into my life and the struggles I was facing. It was a tough season because I did not want to disappoint my parents, but I was also trying to figure out how to own my faith as a college student and young adult and needed their counsel. My parents and I had productive and encouraging conversations. They reminded me how their faith became their own in college and challenged me in areas that I had not thought through before. I am thankful to my parents for showing me mercy and grace and for teaching me how to become an adult and own my faith like never before.

My parents have always been great at probing and checking in to truly understand how I am doing in all areas of life. They have always cared about my heart, my brothers' hearts, and the "why" behind actions and decisions. As a child, there are certain things you do not understand, but as I have grown up, I have learned to appreciate that my parents were constantly displaying the Gospel to me through the way they loved and related to me in my weakness.

Creating a Supportive Home Environment During the Turbulent Teen Years

Questions for Reflection:

1. What are the biggest difficulties my children might have as they enter the teen years?
2. What can I do as a parent to help support, encourage, and guide my teen through these years?
3. What worldly claims do I need to surrender when it comes to my teen? Are my dreams and desires for them biblically informed or based on my own desires?
4. What role does social media play in the life of my teen?
5. How can we better control technology's effect on our family relationships?

Prayer:

Close in prayer for your teen(s) that they would turn to Christ during the many challenges they will face in the years ahead. Ask God how He wants to use you to help guide and support them.

5

Helping Your Teen Own Their Faith

In his book *Marks of the Messenger: Knowing, Living and Speaking the Gospel*, Mack Stiles tells the story of a Brown University student named Kevin Roose who posed as a believer and enrolled at Liberty University as part of an anthropology study of students in the Christian culture. Roose was surprised by how "normal" Christian students were and how easy it was to assimilate with them. He goes on to say, "No one asks me about my faith anymore, so to blend in, I rarely have to do anything more active than keep up my Christian signifiers: going to Bible study, praying before meals, being on time to church. This is what passes for ethical conduct in my world." By the end of the semester, many of his fellow classmates assumed he was a believer[6].

When we read that story, it hit us hard. Our children were in high school and middle school. They had all grown up in a Christian home. They could very easily "play the game" by speaking in Christian terms and participating in Christian activities, yet not truly be following Christ. We feared that they would get the externals right but have hearts that were far from Him. As parents, we need to evaluate how we are parenting so that we are not creating cultural Christians, but rather are helping our children

---

6   Stiles, J Mack. Marks of the Messenger: Knowing, Living and Speaking the Gospel, IVP Books, 2010

become true followers of Christ. We should ensure that our kids are getting the substance of the faith, not just the language of the Christian subculture. There are a few areas of discernment that we need to investigate regarding our children's faith.

Is My Teen's Faith Genuine?

There is no guarantee that children raised in a Christian home will come to faith in Jesus Christ. Only the Lord does the work in the hearts of our children, and it is in His timing when they come to a saving faith in Him. Unfortunately, saying a prayer or making a confession of faith is not a true mark of faith. We must look for signs of true conversion and the work of the indwelling Holy Spirit. We cannot give up hope when our kids seem to be on different time frames in their Christian faith. The best thing we can do, in addition to talking with them and teaching them about the Lord through scripture, is to look for evidence of changes in their lives that reflect their faith and the fruit of the Spirit brought about by salvation.

Is My Teen's Faith Growing?

Secondly, we should look for indications of spiritual growth, faith, and desire/passion for God. Answering the following questions helps gauge where children are in these areas:

- Does my child have a desire for God and His Word?
- Do I see a true conviction of sin and repentance in their lives?
- Who does my child want to hang out with?
- Who and what is my child drawn to?
- Does he/she desire to be with other believers?
- Would Psalm 27:4 describe my child's desire for the Lord?

One thing I ask of the LORD, this is what I seek: that I may dwell in the house of the LORD all the days of my life, to gaze upon the beauty of the LORD and to seek him in his temple.

- Do I observe consistency in their lives and behavior when they are with friends, unbelieving peers, family, and alone?
- Do I see them personally pursuing God?

Having a close relationship with our kids helps us talk to them about their faith, but we need to do so in a humble and unpressured way. Use the time you naturally have with your children, such as when you are preparing dinner and they are in the vicinity, or on a drive together, or just checking in with them before going to bed. Illuminating conversations that pop up organically will feel less intimidating and will deter our desire to hover like a helicopter parent. If you don't have a close relationship with your child and can't imagine having a conversation with him or her about their personal faith, then it's time to enhance your relationship with your child. Spend time with your teen, just enjoying their company and demonstrating your unconditional love by doing something with them that they enjoy. This will give you both the opportunity to build a strong foundation in your relationship.

Is My Teen's Faith Truly Their Own, or are they "Drafting" Off of Mom and Dad?

The third area of discernment is to recognize the blessings and challenges of growing up in a Christian home. It's easy for us to assume our kids have faith in Christ because they actively participate in their Christian family and blend in with Christian society. It can be easy for our kids to spiritually "draft" off of Mom and Dad and not pursue any personal spiritual disciplines, such as personal Bible study, devotions, or prayer, that help them grow in their own faith.

Preparing Your Teen for Challenges to Their Faith

Studies conducted by the Barna Group have found that as many as 64 percent of U.S. 18–29-year-olds who grew up in church have withdrawn from church involvement as adults [7]. In many cases, these young adults began to have doubts and questions about Christianity beginning in middle school or high school. This statistic reiterates the need for parents to be available to their children to help them explore their faith. Studies of those students who remained faithful through high school and college identified two determining factors that really mattered to their owning their faith. The first was regular attendance at church with their parents. The second was knowing and understanding why they believe what they believe. Often, Christian kids are not challenged to think critically about Christianity, how it compares to other world religions, and how it holds up to a secular worldview.

Christian kids need to be knowledgeable about viewpoints that differ and even oppose Christianity in order to become refined in their faith. They need the freedom to ask questions and express doubts about the faith that they have been taught. At these times, parents can help their children by coming alongside them, helping them think through what they believe.

Socially, we have seen many times how kids raised in a Christian home can think they are missing out on all the "fun and excitement" that the world has to offer. It is easy for kids to begin to think that following Christ means they will have a less fulfilling life. We tried to help our kids see through that lie and recognize that true joy in life comes from following Christ. We consulted applicable scriptures and discussed the detriment to the mind, body, and soul of chasing after the fleeting pleasures of the world. We also

---

7   Kinnaman D, Faith for Exiles: 5 Ways for a New Generation to Follow Jesus in Digital Babylon, Baker Books, 2019

shared biblical and secular examples through news outlets with our kids that reiterated this truth.

Shepherding Your Teen into Christian Maturity

As parents, we should redefine what success looks like in the teen years. It is easy to focus on their achievements, the challenges they face, or minimizing bad behavior. We believe that success in the teen years is not good grades and staying out of trouble. It is living and being sold out for Christ, so that it is clear that He is your treasure. If your child is a Christian, we need to lay out the glorious challenge of living for Jesus and advancing His kingdom! We need to be on the offense, not defense!

Ten Ways to Help Your Teens Become Mature in Their Faith

Here are ten practical steps to help our children become mature in their faith:

Practice Gospel-Centered Parenting, Not Legalistic Parenting

Gospel-centered parenting is modeled on Jesus Christ's character and actions. It is sacrificially leading and serving your children with grace and truth. At the center of it is consistently and selflessly loving your children, as Christ loves you, while also speaking the truth of God's Word in love. Humility needs to be at the root of our parenting.

Legalistic parenting focuses on our children's behavior, on following the rules of the home, and on dictating to our kids how they should act, especially around others, to avoid embarrassment for the family. It involves laying down the law without explanation and treating your children conditionally based on how well they succeed or fail at following the rules. Children raised this way tend to have hearts filled with resentment that has built up over time. Pride is often the root of this type of parenting, and it can lead to children who view Christianity as a set of "do's and don'ts." Legalistic parenting overlooks the love of God and the life He offers us in Christ.

<u>Get Theology into Their Hands and Into Their Heads</u>

1. Encourage your teen to seek out a church and youth groups that will help them to think deeply about the things of God. Find a forum, such as a small group of other believers led by a mature Christian, where your kids can figure out their own beliefs and convictions. It is good for our kids to wrestle through their views on doctrine and theology.

2. Go through apologetics (the intellectual defense of the truth of Christianity) books or videos together to help your child think about why they believe what they believe. This will help them personally formulate and defend convictions and reasons for their belief when challenged in a secular classroom or by a friend group. Not all our kids were fond of reading. It helped us get through a book together when our child had their own copies to read, study, highlight, and take notes in. We would both read a chapter a week, then go get coffee to discuss what we had learned. Not only did this feed our faith, but also our relationship through quality time.

3. We also wanted our kids to leave home with a small library of 10-15 books of great theology. Every year at Christmas, we would give them one or two books as gifts.

4. *Appendix A has a list of books that we found helpful to study with our children.*

<u>Promote an Active Devotional Life</u>

When our kids were younger, we did family devotions every night. As they entered the middle school and high school years, their schedules became much busier. We did a few devotions as a family. Otherwise, we did all that we could to encourage our kids to have a regular personal devotion life.

Encourage Your Teen to Regularly Attend Church with the Rest of the Family

Some parents will feel like youth group attendance is enough, but we have seen the value of attending church together as a family. Our kids need to see mom and dad worshiping and following Christ.

Enroll Your Teen in Christian Conferences or Camps

There are several great options for our kids to attend. Boyce College holds an event called D3. Young Life has summer camps, and Summit Ministries holds its Worldview Conferences, just to name a few.

Teach Your Teen to Battle the Temptation and Sin of the Flesh.

While it can be somewhat awkward, it is important to talk with them about purity and battling sexual temptation, even as soon as the early middle school years. A very helpful resource for a parent to study with a same-gender child is a self-guided, personal weekend retreat called "Passport to Purity." [8]

Support Your Teens When They Stand Alone

If your kids are living for Christ, there will be many times when they will stand all alone. As parents, we need to be prepared to come alongside them and encourage them. This may mean long talks or evenings hanging out together.

---

8   For information on Passport to Purity, visit www.familylife.com

Go through the book, *Growing Up Christian: Have You Taken Ownership of Your Relationship with God?*[9] with your teen.

Beginning in eighth grade, Dave would schedule regular Saturday breakfasts with our kids to go through the book. This is a very helpful book for kids to evaluate and own their faith. We would also work through several additional topics that are listed below:

1. Dealing with peer pressure
2. Wisdom in media choices
3. Relating to the opposite sex
4. Developing convictions when it comes to dating
5. Importance of integrity
6. Scriptural view of sexuality and purity
7. False gods
8. Committing to excellence

Appendix B has a list of the questions for each of these topics.

Find a "Wingman" in the Form of a Youth Group Leader or a Pastor

Our kids need to hear from other believers in their lives who care about them. Many of us have benefited greatly from multigenerational mentors who have shared their wisdom and life experiences. We found it to be a huge help and blessing when other mentors imparted truth and encouraged them. Sometimes our children would receive truth from these mentors more readily than from us. We still remember talking to our son about some "great advice" he received from a campus ministry leader that was identical to the advice we had given several months earlier. We laughed after our conversation with him and

9   Graustein, Karl, and Mark Jacobsen. Growing Up Christian: Have You Taken Ownership of Your Relationship with God? P & R Pub. Co., 2005.

were thankful that our son finally heard our advice and that God used his ministry leader to impart what we had tried to share with him.

<u>Make it Fun!</u>

Jim Rayburn, the founder of the teen ministry Young Life, once said, "It is a sin to bore a kid with the gospel." We need to show our kids the true joy in following Jesus.

Reflection on Helping Your Child Own Their Faith by Our Middle Child, Neale.

Growing up in a Christian household, I assumed at an early age that walking with the Lord was the only way to go through life. It was all that I knew, and so why would I even question it? The *what* was very clear: I knew the right things to do, what to say, and how to signal to others that I was a "good person." Decisions seemed black-and-white, with going through the motions being easier than ever. However, I hardly stopped long enough to think through the *why* behind my identity as a Christian. Why did I believe what I did, and how did I have true assurance of my salvation?

Below are three principal traps I faced in making my walk with the Lord my own, along with what my parents did to help me fight in these areas:

1. Making my faith a cultural / family thing.

Ever since I can remember, my family would do devotions and prayer time before bed. These times would often morph into discussions about what it looked like to honor the Lord and live a life devoted to Him. Looking back, these are some of my favorite memories. My parents used this time to emphasize the importance of each of us having a personal relationship with Jesus through our discussions and the questions they asked.

When I was in seventh grade, one of my teachers began mentoring me and asked me one day, "How do you know you are born again?" I had no idea how to answer this. I said the prayer to accept Jesus as my savior, but was this good enough? Was I a Christian, or was this just my family's thing? Is there even a way that we can know we are saved? The realization that maybe I had been latching onto my family for my faith rushed through my head. This teacher began taking me through 1 John, and we examined what it looked like to walk in the light vs. the darkness. We talked about how to have assurance of salvation, and through this, I began to make my faith more of my own.

During this time in seventh grade, I remember my parents walking alongside me as I learned what it looked like to own my faith. The best thing they did was to create a space where I felt comfortable talking about what I was learning around them and processing it with them. I knew with them that I didn't need to be perfect or know all the answers. This freed me up to process and work through 1 John on my own while under their roof and able to share and process what I was learning.

2. Getting caught up in religiosity.

Growing up in the church, I saw very quickly what it looked like to live for the Lord. I observed others in the church living out and growing in the pursuit of their faith. When I was young, I would mimic many of these people's behaviors. I quickly realized how easy it was to signal to others that I was a "good Christian." The insidious part of this was that I made it a competition; how could I show other parents, and more importantly, kids my age, that I was the best Christian? I got wrapped up in doing the right things and giving the correct answers until I was acting just like the Pharisees did: focusing on outward behavior and neglecting the heart.

For us kids, my parents were quick to focus more on our hearts than our actions. They constantly reinforced growing up that God cares more about what is in our hearts than what we do. This created a household where I was not pressured to fit a mold or act a certain way for the sake of externals. It was very clear that my parents never expected me to be perfect; they just wanted me to share their same love for Jesus and to live that out in my life.

In college, a mentor of mine shared with me a short story titled "The Parable of the Fishless Fisherman." The story follows a group of fishermen. They host seminars on catching fish, write books on the technique of fishing, create large buildings dedicated to their fisherman gatherings, and some even go on to get doctorates in "fishing-ology." Yet all the while, no one is fishing. While this story is meant to highlight how easy it is to shy away from making disciples, a secondary takeaway is how easy it is to get caught up in religious activities and think that that is sufficient.

For many of us who have been walking with the Lord for some time, it is far too easy to become a fishless fisherman; we get so caught up in religiosity that we lose sight of our purpose. One thing my parents did to help combat this tendency as I grew up was to push us to get outside of the "holy huddle." This push led us, as kids, to attend a secular high school, where we became friends with people who did not share the same worldview as we did. In becoming friends with people who did not share my faith, the absurdity of getting caught up in religiosity set in, and the simplicity of the great commission came to light.

Over the next several years, my parents were proactive in their communication, asking me how I was growing in my relationship with God, how I was struggling, and whose life I was impacting through my faith. Rather than parenting out of fear by trying to control my decisions or minimizing my exposure to temptation, my parents used their open line of communication and trust to help me grow and navigate through the journey of walking with the Lord in a new environment.

3. Slowly drifting.

When I entered high school and college, I noticed how effortless it was to drift. It was easy to make people think I was fully pursuing the Lord without letting them see the hidden sin and struggles I was dealing with. But at the same time, I was still doing most of the right things, so it was fine to ignore certain parts of my life and make excuses for sin, right? At times, I began to believe I could just coast in certain areas of my faith. After a few years of this, I realized that it is impossible to be idle as a Christian—you are either growing closer to the Lord or farther from him.

By developing personal relationships with us, my parents were able to play a more active role in our lives to encourage us. Growing up, no question was off-limits. My parents had spent years developing trust with us so they could ask us anything. This allowed my parents to have a purposeful dialogue with us when we were drifting in our faith. There were several times when this allowed me to go to my parents with my struggles and have an open discussion with them. My parents approached each of these discussions with love and tenderness. Their demeanors made me feel free to struggle and work through doubts when I was under my parents' roof, further refining my beliefs and convictions before I was on my own. But perhaps the greatest thing my parents did to help me actively grow in my faith was to demonstrate the importance of their daily walks with the Lord. Growing up, my parents would openly read the Bible, pray, and talk about what God was teaching them. This open display of their spiritual disciplines conveyed that they actually practiced what they talked about, making faith all the more real to me.

A mentor of mine once said, "The enemy wants to inoculate us with enough of a disease so that we miss the real cure." This is exactly what Satan tries to do—he tries to convince us that we are fine coasting in our faith and compromising in other areas. Through purposeful parenting, intentional conversations, and showing your kids your personal walk with the Lord, they will see the importance of proactively pursuing their faith and the dangers of slowly drifting away from it.

Helping Your Teen Own Their Faith

Questions for Reflection:

1. At what level is my teen in their relationship with Christ? Is my teen born again and following Christ, or is Christianity more cultural for him/her?
2. In what areas does my teen need to grow spiritually?
3. What can I be doing as a parent to encourage my teen to grow in their faith and to live for Christ?
4. How am I living out the Christian faith in my own life? Am I following Christ? Am I hypocritical... saying one thing and living out another?
5. Who else can help my teen grow in their faith during the teen years? Is there a youth pastor or adult who can disciple my teen?

Prayer:

Pray for the salvation of your teen(s) – that God's spirit would bring about a saving faith in Christ Jesus. If your child is a Christian, pray that they would work in the ways of the Lord and seek to serve Him in every area of their lives.

6

Helping Your Teen be *in* the World but not *of* the World

When our daughter was in eighth grade, her class took a trip to Washington, D.C. During the bus trip, she got into a discussion with a friend who said he was an atheist. He articulated several challenges to Christianity that our daughter had not previously confronted. This was very unnerving for her for two reasons. First, she really liked her friend and was concerned about his soul. Second, she did not feel equipped for the discussion and kept texting us for advice on what to say. This provided a good opportunity for us to help her understand why the Christian faith can be trusted.

Christ called every Christian to be salt and light in this world. That is a difficult challenge for each of us as believers. Even as adults, we struggle with how to be "*in* the world but not *of* it." There have been many times when we as Christians have the fleeting desire to somehow retreat from the world rather than engage with it.

Just think about this past week. All of us have likely struggled with how to best engage our unbelieving neighbors, show love to a challenging family member, or deal with co-workers who are clearly living just for this world. We often wrestle with how best to engage the world on an issue without compromising our faith. Doing so requires a great deal of wisdom, spiritual maturity, and guidance from the Holy Spirit. As parents, we must help our kids learn how to develop skills to engage the lost and impact the culture. Because it is so difficult, we believe this area requires substantial parental coaching and guidance.

Engaging the Culture and the Lost

There were several things we did to help our kids develop the ability to engage non-Christians. The first was that we tried to help them become good evaluators of the many conflicting messages in culture and academia. Our children need to be able to discern and reason through the many ideas coming at them and to evaluate each one through a biblical lens. As Christians, we should be wary of, but not afraid of, the culture. There are many false and deceptive messages coming from culture, but we have the truth of scripture by which we can evaluate the ideas of the world. As believers, we have the words of truth that can withstand any cultural trend, now or in the future. We need to disciple our children so they can actively engage in controversy and not retreat from it.

As parents, we need to think about how to help our kids deal with challenges to their faith from this world. We had many great conversations with our kids as they wrestled through issues of faith, living the Christian life, and engaging society as believers. Many of these discussions not only shaped our children but also stretched us as their parents. These conversations were very rarely planned and often happened in the car, around the dinner table, or late at night. It is important to create an environment in your home where dialogue and questions are welcome and can be discussed. Our kids need to know they can ask us anything without fear of being shut down, shamed, or ignored.

Helping Your Teen See the Beauty of Christ and the Emptiness of the World

The second area is to help them see the beauty of Christ and to see temporal things for what they are. If your child is living for Christ, they will feel like an "oddball," as many of their friends pursue the things that this world falsely promises will bring happiness. It is easy for them to feel like they are missing out when they are sitting at home and "everyone else" is at a party where alcohol is readily available. We had many nights cheering up a child and assuring them that there was nothing wrong with them and that they were not missing out. We also tried to help them see the emptiness and heartbreak that can result from pursuing worldly pleasures. We always tried to live out the Christian life and show them that it can be hard at times, but it always brings the greatest joy to our lives. While they may not have always agreed in the moment, we let them know that it was really others who were missing out on the greater joys we have in Christ. The renowned 20th-century British theologian C.S. Lewis said it best in his sermon, "The Weight of Glory":

> *"The New Testament has lots to say about self-denial, but not about self-denial as an end in and of itself. We are told to deny ourselves and to take up our crosses in order that we may follow Christ; and nearly every description of what we shall ultimately find if we do so contains an appeal to desire. . . . Indeed, if we consider the unblushing promises of reward and the staggering nature of the rewards promised in the Gospels, it would seem that Our Lord finds our desires, not too strong, but too weak. We are half-hearted creatures, fooling about with drink and sex and ambition when infinite joy is offered us, like an ignorant child who wants to go on making mud pies in a slum because he cannot imagine what is meant by the offer of a holiday at the sea. We are far too easily pleased".*[10]

One of the best things we can do as parents is to help

---

10   Lewis, C. S., 1898-1963. The Weight of Glory and Other Addresses. 1st HarperCollins ed. [San Francisco], 2001

our teens realize truth and see the emptiness that results from pursuing worldly pleasures, which lead to unfulfillment and even despair.

Engaging with Purpose to Thrive in a Secular World

Finally, we sought to develop in our children a "missional mindset" for engaging with the world. The approach will differ for each child based on the maturity of their faith. We need to be adept evaluators of our children and know what they can and cannot handle. If they are strong in their faith, we should help them to seek opportunities to engage with non-Christians. If your children attend a secular school, interactions with non-Christians will be a natural part of their day.

How each family chooses to do this may vary widely. We have friends who have sent their children to Christian schools that encourage students to get out into the community and serve in places such as homeless shelters or food banks. This has been a great way for these teens to engage the world alongside other believers. We have also had friends who have homeschooled their children but purposefully placed them into a secular university for additional classes during high school, or have encouraged them to work outside the home for a secular employer. This has been a good opportunity to expose them to very different worldviews while they are still at home. The key is to find what works best for your unique family situation and each child's needs.

Our eldest son was homeschooled for a short time, then attended Christian schools up until high school. At that point, we felt he was strong enough in his faith to go to a secular school. At the same time, we wanted to put him in a situation that would push him out of his comfort zone, refining him and strengthening his faith — while still under our roof. After his first day of freshman year, Josh jumped in the car and immediately said, "I have nothing in common with these kids. I feel like a fish out of water." As a parent, this was hard to hear—but not unexpected. That first semester was a rough one. He endured crude locker room talk as a member of the basketball team. At one point, he was directly asked by a teammate, in front of the whole team, which porn sites he visited. When our son replied that he didn't look at porn, several of the boys burst into laughter and only quieted down when another boy defended our son, saying that it was okay that he didn't look at porn.

The semester continued to have its challenges, but our son did find a small group of upperclassmen who were involved in a Christian organization for high school students called Student Venture (now known as CRU). It helped him to connect with them, even though they were three years older. Still, our son felt very alone at school, and over winter break, he came to us requesting a transfer to a Christian school. We talked through his reasons for wanting to transfer. We reviewed his semester together, even though we had been having ongoing talks with him about the daily challenges he experienced throughout the semester. After our discussion with him, we all decided to pray about his school situation for 48 hours, and then come back together to see how the Lord was leading each one of us. Our son concluded that he felt the Lord calling him to stay in his secular school and to be mission-minded in his interactions with his classmates.

In his sophomore year, he invited more people to come to Student Venture. Through God's grace, by the end of that school year, the group grew from five students to 40 students (10% of his high school) attending regularly.

Reflection on Being In, but not Of the World, by Our Oldest, Josh.

My family and I often talk of an illuminating experience when we realized one evening that my siblings and I could name no close friends who didn't identify as Christians.

Between our heavy involvement at church and our enroll-ment at a small Christian school, we realized that we had become largely inactive in engaging the world and advancing the Kingdom of God. Over the years, we had slowly grown too comfortable living in our Christian "bubble," surround-ed by a safe community of like-minded individuals. After that conversation, we realized it was time for a change. My parents and I prayerfully considered sending me to a high school that was radically different than the Christian education I had grown used to. While I was initially scared and opposed to the idea, God made it abundantly clear to all of us that this was the direction he was leading us.

What did I experience?

The next year, as I entered high school, it felt like being thrown in the deep end of a swimming pool after only one swimming lesson. I had a little practice and knowledge, but no experience. It was hard. The initial days and weeks felt like years. Friendships were much more challenging to form. Conversations in the locker rooms were startling. I felt alone and isolated. I had trouble connecting with others and feeling like I could be myself. After a hard first semester of my freshman year, I considered transferring to a local Christian school. I hoped that finally I could experience the comfort of a like-minded community again. But God made it clear that he wanted me to stay.

Growing up surrounded by modern American Christi-anity left me with a worldview that there are two opposing cultures: Christian culture and worldly culture. Culture is defined as "the attitudes and behavioral characteristics of a particular social group." As I left the Christian "bubble" I had grown up in, I began to see the dangers of a super-ficial cultural Christianity that had become more focused on creating an ecosystem of specific attitudes, rules, and behaviors, and less on the active pursuit of the heart of Je-sus. I quickly saw how this culture had led to two negative effects, and I had to surrender them to the Lord. The first was an implicit disdain and superiority that I felt towards the world. The second was a concentration on protection and preservation that neutralized my impact on the world.

As I progressed through high school, I was exposed to another culture: the world. A chaotic and confusing worldview focused on self-sufficiency, self-actualization, and self-indulgence, with its highest ideal being self-authenticity. I saw only emptiness at the end of living for oneself. These two worldviews oppose one another, but there is a third point of view. That is the culture of Grace found in the gospel. Grace is the heart of the Gospel of Jesus Christ. Everything changed for me when I began to recognize the abundant, incalculable depth of God's grace for me. I found freedom and a radically changed perspective on God's purpose for me. I saw the world and others through the lens of Jesus' heart—a desire for all to be saved and a tenderness towards the blindness and brokenness of those living apart from God. The questions I asked myself changed from "Are my friends influencing me negatively?" to "Am I communicating the heart of God in my interactions?" and from "How can I prove Christianity is right?" to "Am I sharing that there isn't just a right way of living, but there is a better way in which my friends can find freedom?"

As my parents described earlier in this chapter, the Spirit of God worked powerfully in my remaining years in high school. I saw the transformation that can only occur when God works through us. He brought restoration and renewal to many students in my high school, and I had the joy of sitting in the front row as He did the work.

How did my parents help?

Throughout these formative years, my parents were there to support me every step of the way. My parents took a risk in taking me out of Christian education. They invited me to consider how I can make an impact outside of my comfortable Christian bubble and influence others for Christ. My parents walked alongside me as I wrestled with how to engage the world. Looking back, it was my parents' communication and conduct that helped provide the encouragement and guidance I needed.

In my parents' communication, they kept an open dialogue, helping me process the challenges I was facing, and welcoming my doubts and concerns. They found regular opportunities to communicate with respect and authenticity, and to share their hearts. They reminded me of their unconditional love and communicated with grace, tenderness, and patience. They didn't act shocked or surprised by the ugliness of the world I was encountering, and I felt free to share openly what I was experiencing. This helped me live with integrity, being honest about the hardships and joys of engaging the world for Jesus. They had high expectations of me, allowing me to live out the call of 1 Timothy 4:12: "Let no one despise you for your youth, but set the believers an example in speech, in conduct, in love, in faith, in purity."

Finally, my parents' conduct modeled their values. They displayed love for others, demonstrated genuine faith, and had a curiosity about the harder questions of the faith. They exemplified integrity and served me in extraordinary ways, giving me a blueprint for sacrificially loving those around me. They stepped into the unknown and the uncomfortable, encouraging me to do the same.

Helping Your Teen be in the World but not of the World

Questions for Reflection:

1. How does God want to use our teens for His Kingdom?
2. What can I/we do to help my teen develop their own convictions, informed by the scriptures?
3. How am I helping my child to reach the lost and be missionally minded?

Prayer:

Pray that God would both protect your teens from the evils of this world and use them to reach their peers for Christ.

7

A Biblical Case Study and Application for the "Second Half"

Leaders Not Followers (A Case Study of the Old Testament Book of Daniel)

We should challenge our kids to be leaders, not followers. Too often, we have low expectations for youth today and do not encourage them to high standards. They are capable of much more than we give them credit for. This should not be imposing our will or dreams on our children, but rather working with them to find things they enjoy doing. We have seen far too many parents have dreams for their kids and then try to force them to conform to their desires. As parents, we should help our kids find their own dreams, and then come alongside them to help them achieve what God has called them to do.

A Case Study of Four Teens Set Loose in a Pagan Society

Young people can have a tremendous impact on society, both positive and negative. We should never underestimate the power of the words and actions of an influential person on others. God used Daniel to influence the pagan kings of Babylon throughout most of his lifetime. His life and doctrine were congruent as he worshiped and lived for God.

The first chapter of Daniel describes how Daniel and his three friends, Shadrach, Meshach, and Abednego, faithfully lived for God in a pagan society. Let's take a closer look:

Daniel 1:1-21 says:

In the third year of the reign of Jehoiakim king of Judah, Nebuchadnezzar king of Babylon came to Jerusalem and besieged it. And the Lord gave Jehoiakim, king of Judah, into his hand, with some of the vessels of the house of God. And he brought them to the land of Shinar, to the house of his god, and placed the vessels in the treasury of his god. Then the king commanded Ashpenaz, his chief eunuch, to bring some of the people of Israel, both of the royal family and of the nobility, youths without blemish, of good appearance and skillful in all wisdom, endowed with knowledge, understanding, learning, and competent to stand in the king's palace, and to teach them the literature and language of the Chaldeans. The king assigned them a daily portion of the food that the king ate, and of the wine that he drank. They were to be educated for three years, and at the end of that time they were to stand before the king. Among these were Daniel, Hananiah, Mishael, and Azariah of the tribe of Judah. And the chief of the eunuchs gave them names: Daniel he called Belteshazzar, Hananiah he called Shadrach, Mishael he called Meshach, and Azariah he called Abednego. But Daniel resolved that he would not defile himself with the king's food, or with the wine that he drank. Therefore he asked the chief of the eunuchs to allow him not to defile himself. And God gave Daniel favor and compassion in the sight of the chief of the eunuchs, and the chief of the eunuchs said to Daniel, "I fear my lord the king, who assigned your food and your drink; for why should he see that you were in worse condition than the youths who are of your own age? So you would endanger my head with the king."

Then Daniel said to the steward whom the chief of the eunuchs had assigned over Daniel, Hananiah, Mishael, and Azariah, "Test your servants for ten days; let us be given vegetables to eat and water to drink. Then let our appearance and the appearance of the youths who eat the king's food be observed by you, and deal with your servants according to what you see." So he listened to them in this matter, and tested them for ten days. At the end of ten days it was seen that they were better in appearance and fatter in flesh than all the youths who ate the king's food. So the steward took away their food and the wine they were to drink, and gave them vegetables.

As for these four youths, God gave them learning and skill in all literature and wisdom, and Daniel had understanding in all visions and dreams. At the end of the time, when the king had commanded that they should be brought in, the chief of the eunuchs brought them in before Nebuchadnezzar. And the king spoke with them, and among all of them none was found like Daniel, Hananiah, Mishael, and Azariah. Therefore they stood before the king. And in every matter of wisdom and understanding about which the king inquired of them, he found them ten times better than all the magicians and enchanters that were in all his kingdom. And Daniel was there until the first year of King Cyrus.
The Holy Bible, English Standard Version® (ESV®)

From this passage, we read that Israel was taken captive by Babylon. Babylon's King Nebuchadnezzar ordered that youths from the royal and noble families of Israel be brought into his court to learn the culture, laws, and customs of Babylon. It is estimated that Daniel and his friends were between 14 and 16 years old at the time.

The king wanted to take the best and brightest of the Israelite youth and submerge them in the Babylonian culture, intending to convert them into Babylonians. He had a specific agenda with purposeful, detailed steps to educate them and fully absorb them into society, including giving them new names.

Today's secular society has an agenda for our children as well. The way our children are educated in secular schools, what they are exposed to in the media, and how they are influenced by their peers can all lean heavily away from Christian principles.

Daniel and his friends were taken in their youth to a pagan kingdom, away from their families and Godly influences. At this point, these young men had to decide for whom they were going to live. Based on their response, they must have been raised in the instruction and knowledge of the Torah (the first five books of the Bible), so they were able to wisely and faithfully compare the Word of God with the Babylonian teachings. These four young men chose to live for and to serve God while in their captivity.

Our children will face similar decisions as they engage with secular society. Who will they serve? It is essential that, before they are released into the world, they are equipped with the knowledge of God's Word and apply it to their lives so they are prepared and can remain faithful to God in a fallen society. While Daniel, Shadrach, Meshach, and Abednego were abruptly thrust into Babylon, ideally, our children should be gradually exposed to the secular world. Our role is to teach and equip them as they interact with those who don't share their beliefs. As parents, we need to be available to help them navigate this world.

When entering secular society, our kids will be faced with many chances to engage in sinful behavior. For them, it will be decision time. Who will they live for? How will they make their decisions? The teen years are a fertile time for our children to learn and grow as they leave childhood and move toward adulthood, to learn how to make good decisions that impact them and others. It is also a time for them to learn lessons from poor decisions that have negative impacts. They should do this while still under the safety of Mom and Dad's roof, so that parents can help guide them through decision-making informed by the scriptures. The teen years will reveal to parents the true strength or weakness of their relationships with their kids. The relationship must be strong in order to best navigate these years together. If the relationship is weak, it is the parents' responsibility to lovingly and humbly pursue their child in order to connect so that the child knows he or she is loved in a way that helps prepare them to face the world.

The family must become a harbor in the storm and a safe haven that is always welcoming. Several times, our children would say, ``You guys are my only friends right now." While that was hard to hear, we were thankful to have that relationship with them. We tried to make our home a fun and welcoming place. We encouraged our teens to have their friends over and to invite kids over that they wanted to get to know better. This allowed us to know their friends and support our kids in life-giving relationships. It helped that Daniel had like-minded friends who were living out their convictions with him, and our children will benefit from having like-minded friends to walk with in life. However, this may ebb and flow over the years, and there will be seasons when our kids will feel alone as believers. It is then that the family needs to support them and encourage them, reminding them that they are never alone. God will never leave nor forsake them.

Having a good relationship with our children helped them handle peer pressure well, but sometimes, they still succumbed to it. In those cases, our open relationship made it possible for them to come to us, share their sin, repent, and ask us to hold them accountable.

Our kids will face many external pressures and influences from peers, such as cursing, lying, watching unwholesome movies, substance abuse, giving in to sexual temptation, and more. A great way to prepare our kids is to proactively discuss probable difficult scenarios ahead of time, before they are actually faced with them. An example of this is talking with your child about what their actions will be if they end up at a party where underage drinking is occurring. Help them decide in advance what they will say and do if asked to participate. Ask them if they will be tempted to join in with their peers. Talk through how their reaction to peer pressure will impact them and other people, now and in the future. Discuss with them how they can participate in secular activities while remaining faithful to God and His Word.

From society's perspective, Daniel and his friends had an enviable position. The King ensured that they would receive the best education, be trained for a position of power, and eat from the King's table. He even had their names changed to reflect their full acceptance into the kingdom.

The youths accepted three out of four things the king offered. They could participate in the Babylonian education, for they had already been fully educated in their own doctrine. They could be trained for positions of influence, for they would know Babylonian customs but could influence the culture from a God-centered worldview. They even accepted new Babylonian names because their identity was not in a name, but in the one true God, Yahweh.

In verse 8, we see them rejecting the fourth offer by not accepting the food from the King's table. As Israelites, they could not defile themselves by eating or drinking from the King's table, because much of the food most likely had been offered to pagan gods and did not meet the dietary guidelines required in the Torah. When faced with this dilemma, they had to choose whom they would serve: God or man. They resolved in advance on their course of action.

Notice how they handled this dilemma. They did not draw attention to themselves, but respectfully approached the head eunuch to make the request for vegetables instead of the King's food. They offered the reasonable expectation that, if they did not thrive as much as those eating the King's food, they would submit to whatever the head eunuch decided to do with them as a result. When it was obvious that they appeared better and fatter on vegetables than on the King's food, the steward let them continue this diet. After all, his only concern was that they improve under his care so that it would be a good reflection on his stewardship of them and keep him in favor with the King.

We also need to help our kids critique and see culture through a Christian lens. We should discuss how culture influences us through education, news, social media, and peer pressure.

We need to help our kids have a longer, eternal view of life by *teaching them about the benefits of righteousness.* This is not easy for a teenager to grasp. They know they will gain popularity and acceptance if they adopt the values of their peers and society. They also know that they may be ostracized if they don't. Approval of God is infinitely more rewarding than the approval of the crowd. 1 Peter 3:14-17 tells us, "*... even if you should suffer for the sake of righteousness, you are blessed. And do not fear their intimidation, and do not be troubled, but sanctify Christ as Lord in your hearts ... For it is better, if God should will it so, that you should suffer for doing what is right rather than for doing what is wrong.*" Talk with your children about the benefits of obedience and the cost of conformity.

Finally, *teach your kids the fear of God.* The 18th-century minister John Witherspoon said, "It is only the fear of God that can deliver us from the fear of men." And Proverbs 16:6 tells us, "*... by the fear of the Lord one keeps away from evil.*" If your child develops a reverential awe of God as he learns about God's attributes, his desire to please Him will overcome his fear of what others think of him.

Your kids can have an impact on this world. The King brought Daniel to Babylon to change him, but Daniel ended up changing Babylon. Our kids can have that same impact today.

A Biblical Case Study and Application for the "Second Half"

Questions for Reflection:

Spend this last week reflecting individually, or as a couple if you are married, on your weekly reflections. Pick two to three things that you believe will have the greatest impact on your child during the teen years and list those below:

1____

____

____

2____

____

3.____

____

____

Now list specific actions (with due dates) you can take, beginning tomorrow.

Action	Frequency	Due Date
1.		
2.		
3.		
4.		

Epilogue

We wrote this book because we have benefited greatly from the tremendous Godly wisdom of other parents over the years. Shortly before we were going to have children, we asked Christian couples we admired for advice on raising children. While there were quite a few differences in the answers, they all had two themes:

1. Love God, and be a parent who earnestly seeks to follow Christ.
2. Invest in your relationship with your kids, and model/teach Christian living as you live life together.

As we were in the "thick of parenting," it was helpful to remember that our main job was not to get them into a great college or to chauffeur them to and from sporting events and other extracurricular activities, but to love God and follow Him. Our job is not to "fix" our kids or pressure them to be Christians; only God can do that. Our job is to love God and follow him, model that for our kids, and love our kids with the love Christ has shown us.

When Christ was asked, "Which is the greatest commandment in the Law?" Jesus replied: "'Love the Lord your God with all your heart and with all your soul and with all your mind.' This is the first and greatest commandment. And the second is like it: 'Love your neighbor as yourself.' All the Law and the Prophets hang on these two commandments." (Matthew 22:36-40).

This simplicity of focus is very freeing from the myriad of rules and regulations that the religious rulers in Jesus' time believed would save us. We pray you have the same simplicity of focus as you navigate the teen years with your children.

Appendix A: Suggested Reading for Your Kids

<u>Books we encouraged our kids to read
and take to college:</u>

- Dietrich Bonhoeffer, *The Cost of Discipleship*
- John Bunyan, *The Pilgrim's Progress*
- Elisabeth Elliot, *Through Gates of Splendor*
- Karl Graustein, *Growing Up Christian*
- Kent Hughes, *Disciplines of a Godly Man*
- Tim Keller, *The Reason for God*
- C.S. Lewis, *Mere Christianity*
- Paul Little, *Know What You Believe*
- J.I. Packer, *Knowing God*
- Nancy Pearcey, *Total Truth*
- David Platt, *Radical*
- R.C. Sproul, *The Holiness of God*
- John Stott, *Basic Christianity*
- Lee Strobel, *The Case for Faith*
- Don Whitney, *Spiritual Disciplines for the Christian Life*

Appendix B: Topics and Questions For Weekly Breakfasts with your Kids

Breakfast 1: Dealing with Peer Pressure

1. Look up I Cor 15:33. Why is this true? When have you seen this happen
2. Read the verse and list the principle

Verse	Principle
Prov 1:10.15	
Prov 2:10-12,20	
Psalm 1	
Prov 4:14,15	
Prov 13:20	
Prov 20:19	

Based on these verses...
3. How should you select friends?
4. When should you disassociate
5. Who should influence your life most?

Breakfast 2: Wisdom in Media Choices

1. What is the world's purpose of media? What is God's?
2. What would Christ watch/read in the media? How would he decide?
3. How does what we watch affect us?
4. What will you do if...
    - Watching TV, and a bad commercial comes on?
    - You are at a friend's house, and they want to watch a really popular R-rated movie?

Breakfast 3: Relating to the Opposite Sex

1. How should a husband treat his wife? (Read 1 Peter 3:7 & Eph 5:22-33)
2. Why did God create Eve? (Gen 2:18-25)

Read Gen 2:18-25 and answer the following:
3. What is the basis of Adam's acceptance of Eve?
4. What relationship does God want for a husband & wife?
5. Should everyone be married? (1 Cor 7:7-9)
6. How should young men treat young women? Why?

Breakfast 4: Developing Convictions When it Comes to Dating

1. What should be the main purpose or goal of going on a date?
2. What exactly is a date, and how is it different from just hanging out as friends?
3. What qualities and characteristics should you look for when choosing someone to date?
4. How should a Christian's faith shape the way they approach dating and relationships?

5. How should 2 Corinthians 6:14–15 guide who you choose to date?"

Breakfast 5: Importance of Integrity

1. What is integrity?
2. How did David show integrity? (1 Sam 26:1-12, 1 Sam 24:1-17)
3. Can we trust our heart/feelings (Jer 17:9)
4. List principles of integrity (Prov 4:20-27)
5. What is lying? Why is it so dangerous?
6. What are we to do in communication? (Eph 4:25)

Breakfast 6: Scriptural View of Sexuality and Purity

1. Why did God create sex? Read Gen 1:27&28, Gen 4:1 (in KJV), Prv 5:19, 1 Cor 6:9, Matt 15:18-19
2. Purpose of a kiss?
3. Purpose of holding hands?
4. Why is sex outside marriage wrong?
5. What is purity? (list scriptures you find)
6. What should purity look like for you personally? (Limits, areas of temptation, etc.)
7. Write out your own Purity covenant.

Breakfast 7: False Gods

1. How are we to love God? Matt 22
2. How would you define an idol?
3. List idols in these scriptures:
    - Eph 5:5
    - Phil 3:19
    - Gal 5:19-21
4. What are some idols you see people around you pursuing?
5. What idols do you struggle with most?

Breakfast 8: Committing to Excellence

1. Read Col 3:17. How should this affect our work?
2. What is the result of God's work? (list verses to support)

3. How are we to treat the gifts & abilities God has given us? Read Matt 25:14-30
4. Read Jonathan Edwards' resolutions (https://www.jonathan-edwards.org/Resolutions.html). How old was he when he wrote them?
5. Write your own resolutions that you want to commit to as you enter adulthood.